· BIG BOOK OF ·
SCROLL SAW
PUZZLES

More Than 75 Easy-to-Cut Designs in Wood

Tony & June Burns

A Scroll Saw Woodworking & Crafts Book
www.ScrollSawer.com

FOX CHAPEL
PUBLISHING

Dedication

We dedicate this book to our parents, for their endless love and support made this book possible.

Acknowledgments

We would like to thank the following individuals and companies who have helped make this book possible.

Jeremy Burns, our son and an exceptional artist
Alan Giagnocavo of Fox Chapel Publishing Co. Inc.
Chuck Olson of Olson Blades
Ray Seymore of SEYCO
R. Stroulger of Hobbies (Dereham) Limited-England
Ernie Mellon of Eclipse Scroll Saw Company

To learn more about the other great books from Fox Chapel Publishing, or to find a retailer near you, call toll-free 800-457-9112 or visit us at *www.FoxChapelPublishing.com*.

Note to Authors: We are always looking for talented authors to write new books. Please send a brief letter describing your idea to Acquisition Editor, 1970 Broad Street, East Petersburg, PA 17520.

Printed in China
First printing

Foreword

We started out in 1984. Tony was teaching Industrial Arts and I was a new mom. We wanted a way to supplement our income in the summer when Tony wasn't teaching. I loved to paint and draw. So with Tony's woodworking experience and my art background, we combined our talents.

Working with wood, we designed and made everything from weather vanes to candle sconces and sold them at local shows. Tony, being as frugal as he is, could not throw away even the smallest of leftover scraps. We designed several small art puzzles utilizing these "scraps," and thus began our puzzle venture. We enjoy designing our scroll saw puzzles and being unique in our field.

Now, more than thirty years later, we are even busier. We have four children who inspire us daily with their ideas and interests, and we still enjoy exhibiting our work at shows in the northeast.

In addition is our love for the foot-powered machinery that we have collected over the years. We enjoy bringing machines to shows to demonstrate and share a bit of history and our passion for scrolling with others.

— Tony and June Burns

Contents

54 | Down on the Farm

90 | Holidays

Getting Started

So you've decided to become a puzzle maker—hooray! We welcome you to this fun and challenging art. To get started, check out these tips and tricks. You'll learn some scroll saw basics as well as some of our personal preferences. Safety is always our top priority, but we hope these hints will also make the process easy and fun!

Choosing Wood

When purchasing wood for puzzle making, we suggest that you buy the best grade of wood you can afford. Look for wood with a straight grain and few defects. Also, avoid lumber that appears damp or heavier than usual.

We prefer to use silver maple, poplar, basswood, and pine. These woods are relatively easy to find and for beginners to cut. Denser types of wood and plywood are stronger but are harder to cut. We have also had fairly good success with 19mm solid-core Baltic birch. We have a great love for oak and butternut, the latter being easier to cut. These harder woods, including Baltic birch, tend to dull blades faster, but they add fun and challenges to a great project. Your local supplier may have these or other varieties from which to choose.

Choose wood that is at least ¾" (19mm) thick, but no thicker than 1" (25mm). For some of our larger puzzles, you can use up to 1¼" (32mm)-thick wood. If you are planning to paint your puzzle, use something like pine or basswood with very little grain. Choose a nicer hardwood, like cherry or maple, if you want to stain the puzzle or leave it natural. Use caution with highly figured hardwoods; the grain can be distracting if it doesn't work with the pattern design.

Choosing Blades

Use larger blades (higher numbers) as the thickness or the density (hardness) of the wood increases. A rule of thumb is to use a #5 or #7 blade for ¾" to 1" (19mm to 25mm)-thick medium-hard wood (such as cherry, walnut, or maple). Larger blades (#9 and up) are more durable. They are also less likely to break as you apply pressure, and they cut faster. They are mandatory for especially thick or hard wood.

Use smaller blades (#3 and smaller) for thin wood. These blades cut more slowly, which gives you additional control when cutting thin wood. Puzzle cutters sometimes use smaller blades to make tight turns, but for general scrolling, a #2/0 blade is small enough. Choose the blade that will allow you to cut the smallest frets without breaking every few cuts.

Consider the intricacy of the cuts. Larger blades will not cut tight corners or fit into small frets. When cutting intricate projects, choose the smallest blade that will cut the thickness of wood.

Attaching and Removing Patterns

Temporary-bond spray adhesive is the most common method used to attach patterns to stock. Cover the wood blank with painter's tape to lubricate the blade and make the pattern easier to remove. Photocopy the pattern. Spray the adhesive on the back of the copy of the pattern, wait a few seconds, and then press the pattern onto the taped blank. Rubber cement or glue sticks work similarly.

Some scrollers prefer to use clear adhesive shelf paper. Place a piece onto the table, shiny side up. Apply spray adhesive to the back of the pattern, and attach it to the shelf paper. Cut the pattern pieces out. To apply them to the blanks, peel the liner off the shelf paper.

You can also use graphite transfer paper. Place the pattern on the blank and slip a sheet of transfer paper in between the pattern and the blank. Use a few pieces of painter's tape to hold the pattern and transfer paper in place. Trace around the pattern with a red pen (so you know where you have traced). Choose a light-colored transfer paper for darker wood. Carbon paper costs less than graphite paper, but must be sanded off before finishing.

A quick wipe of mineral spirits will remove most adhesives left behind on the wood. Commercial adhesive removers work as well.

Cover a blank with painter's tape, and then use spray adhesive or a glue stick to attach the pattern. The tape is easy to peel off the wood when you are done cutting.

Sawing Tips

SQUARING THE TABLE

Most scroll saws have an adjustable table that allows you to make cuts at different angles. There are times when you want the saw set at an angle, but most cutting is done with the blade perpendicular to the table. If the table is even slightly off square, the cuts will be angled, which will prevent the puzzle pieces from sliding together properly.

The most common method for squaring a table uses a small metal square, or right-angle tool. Set the square flat on the saw table against a blade that has been inserted and tensioned. Adjust the table to form a 90° angle to the blade.

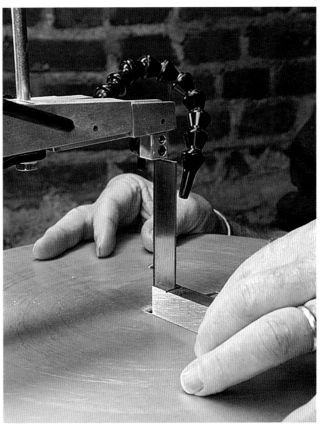

Squaring the table is essential to puzzle making. An easy way to check the table angle is to use a small metal square.

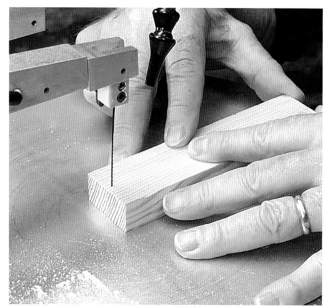

Check the angle of your table with the kerf-test method. Simply cut a piece of wood, rotate it, and see if the blank fits in the kerf. If it fits, your table is square.

The cutting-through method is also popular. Saw through a piece of scrap wood at least ¾" (19mm) thick and check the angle of the cut using a square. Adjust the table until you get a perfectly square cut.

You can also use the kerf-test method. Take a 1¾" (44mm)-thick piece of scrap wood and cut about ½" (13mm) into it. Stop the saw, back the blade out, and spin the wood around to the back of the blade. If the blade slips easily into the kerf, the table is square. If it doesn't slide into the kerf, adjust the table and perform the test again until the blade slips in easily.

BLADE TENSION

Before inserting a blade, completely remove the tension. Clamp both ends of the blade into the blade holders and adjust the tension. Push on the blade with your finger. It should flex no more than ⅛" (3mm) forward, backward, or side-to-side.

A blade that does not have enough tension will wander. It will also flex from side to side, making for irregular or angled cuts. If you press too hard on a loose blade, it will usually snap. A blade that has too much tension is more susceptible to breaking and tends to pull out of the blade holders. In general, it is better to make the blade too tight than too loose.

Safety Tips

- Read and follow the manufacturer's suggested operating safety guidelines provided with your machine. If you do not have these, contact the manufacturer and get them.

- Protect your eyes with glasses, goggles, or similar equipment.

- Remove any loose clothing or jewelry before you operate the saw. If you have long hair, tie it back.

- Work in a well-ventilated area. Consider using a mask, an air cleaner, a dust collector, or any combination of these to protect your lungs from fine dust.

- Be sure that the work area is well lighted.

- Keep your hands a safe distance away from the blade.

- Don't work when you are tired or unfocused.

BLADE-ENTRY HOLES

Some patterns have blade-entry holes marked. If the pattern doesn't, place the hole near a line to be cut to prolong the blade life, but don't place the hole on a curving line or inside corner (if possible). Drill the hole perpendicular to the blank. Use a drill press if you have one; otherwise, use a hand drill and make the holes as vertical as possible. Drill through the blank into scrap wood to prevent tear out on the backside of the blank. If you have the space, use a larger bit—it will make it easier to thread the blades through. For thin veining cuts, use the smallest bit the blade will fit through.

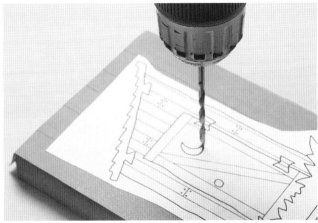

Place the blade-entry holes at a point or corner. If that's not possible, place entry holes as close as possible to the cutting line.

Painting and Finishing

Before you begin painting, make sure to sand the front, back, and edges of the puzzle with 100- to 150-grit sandpaper. Then, mix acrylic paint with water to make a wash. Apply the wash with a small paintbrush or cloth. If you'd like a more natural finish, you can dip your puzzle in boiled linseed oil and let it dry. If desired, apply a couple of coats of spray finish to your puzzle.

Materials and Tools

These are the materials and tools you'll need for each puzzle project.

MATERIALS:
- Pine, ½" (13mm) to ¾" (19mm) thick: size varies
- Spray adhesive
- Sandpaper: 100 to 150 grit
- Acrylic paint

TOOLS:
- Blades: #5 skip-tooth, #2 skip-tooth
- Sanding block
- Paintbrushes

Making a Puzzle Step-by-Step

This pansy puzzle is a great first puzzle to scroll, sand, and paint. It's challenging for a beginner, but it's also satisfying for the experienced scroller.

We used pine for this project, but we also like to use silver maple, poplar, and basswood for puzzles. A good rule of thumb is to look for wood with a straight grain and few defects. The grain on the pansy should run horizontally.

1 **Begin cutting the puzzle outline.** Attach or transfer the pattern to the wood. Begin cutting with a #5 skip-tooth blade at the bottom right corner, and cut to point A. Sharply rotate the blank to avoid a rounded corner.

2 **Finish cutting the puzzle outline.** Cut to point B. Gently back out, making sure to keep the saw running as you do. Pivot the wood on the blade to make a sharp turn, and continue to point C. Repeat the pivots at points C and D, and then finish cutting the perimeter. Discard the waste.

3 **Cut piece #1.** Use a #2 skip-tooth blade. There is a sharp angle at the center of this cut; carefully pivot to avoid breakage. At the exit point, slow down. This will prevent the end grain from ripping or tearing. Remove piece #1 and set it aside.

4 **Cut the remaining pieces.** Cut through piece #2 to reach piece #3. When you have completed the cut, remove piece #3 and set it aside. At point A, cut out piece #2 where it joins piece #4. There are two points where you will enter and gently back out. Remove piece #2 and set it aside. Make the three detail cuts in piece #4. Gently back out of each cut.

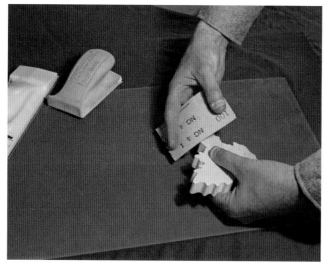

5 **Sand the pieces.** Remove the pattern. Use a 100- to 150-grit sanding pad to sand the front and back of the puzzle. Make sure to sand with the grain. Then, sand the edges of the puzzle with a downward motion.

6 **Paint the pieces.** Mix acrylic paint with water to form a wash. Take the puzzle apart and paint each piece separately. Dip a small brush or cloth into the paint and wipe it onto the puzzle in the direction of the grain. Wipe off any excess paint with a clean, dry cloth.

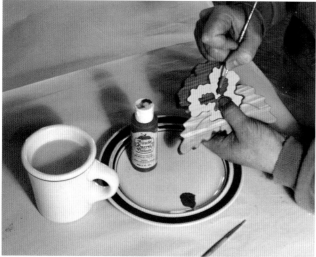

7 **Add the details.** Allow the pieces to dry fully, and then add the details with full-strength acrylic paints and a fine brush. If desired, spray the completed pieces with several light coats of clear matte finish.

Pansy

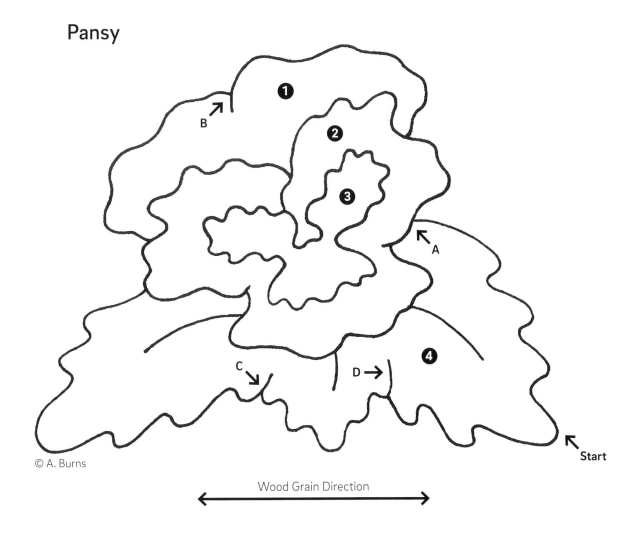

© A. Burns

Wood Grain Direction

Noah's Ark

On the following pages, you'll find patterns for
Noah's ark, complete with Mr. and Mrs. Noah,
trees, and animals. We've included horses,
elephants, bunnies, and even unicorns. All of
the patterns are to be used at 100%. When you
and your kids aren't playing with these puzzles,
arrange them to make an attractive display.

You can make a base for the ark from a
¾" by 3" by 8" (19mm by 76mm by 203mm) piece
of wood. Cut a dado lengthwise down the center
that is the same thickness as the ark (¾" or 19mm).
Do not dado more than ⅜" (10mm) deep.

18 Sign of Hope

20 Jungle Royalty

26 Grazing Horses

16 Noah's Ark
17 Mr. and Mrs. Noah

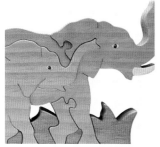

21 Traveling Elephants

22 Gentle Giants

24 Deer in Glen

25 Hoppy Bunnies

28 Kangaroo Pair

29 Penguins on Ice

30 Unicorns

31 Turtle Family

32 Cypress Tree

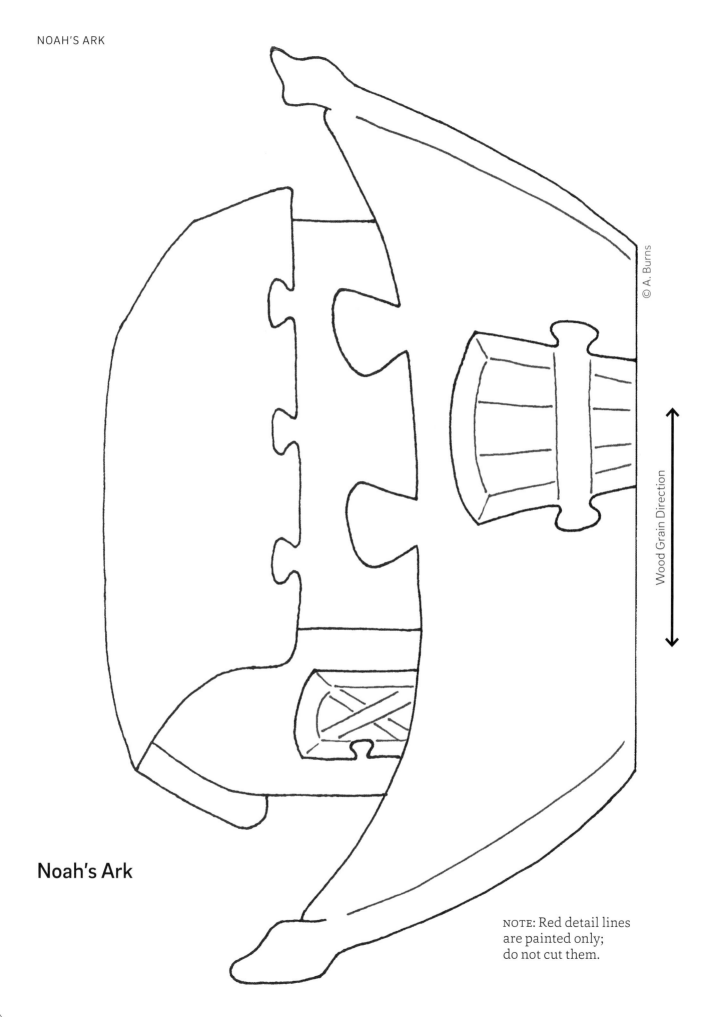

© A. Burns

Wood Grain Direction

Noah's Ark

NOTE: Red detail lines are painted only; do not cut them.

Mr. and Mrs. Noah

Wood Grain Direction

© A. Burns   © A. Burns

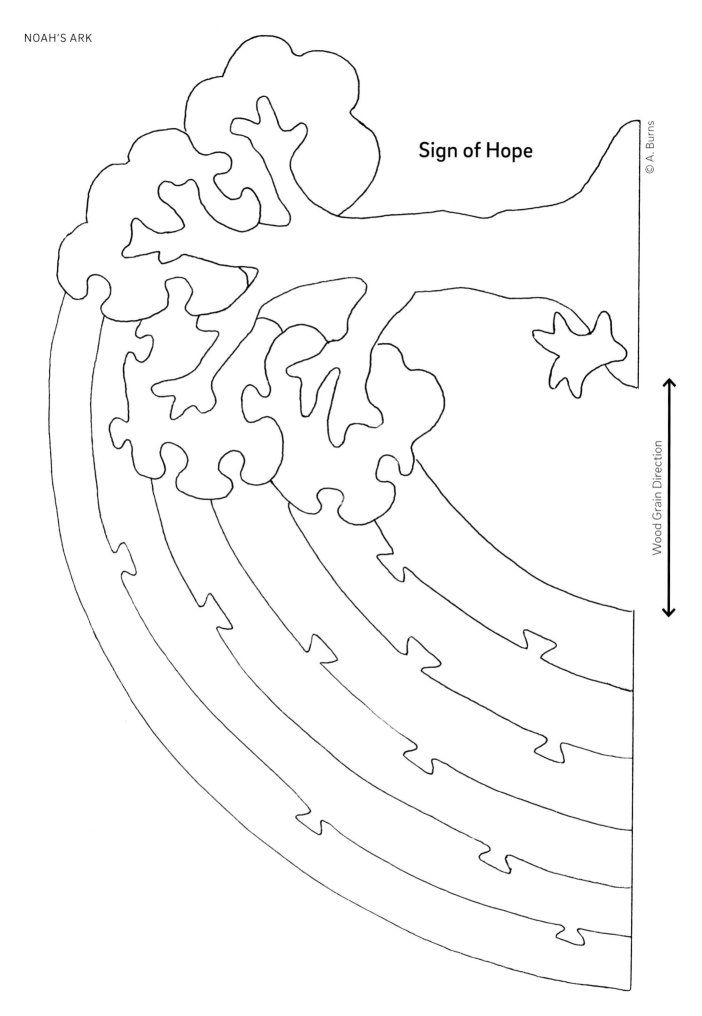

Sign of Hope

© A. Burns

Wood Grain Direction

Jungle Royalty

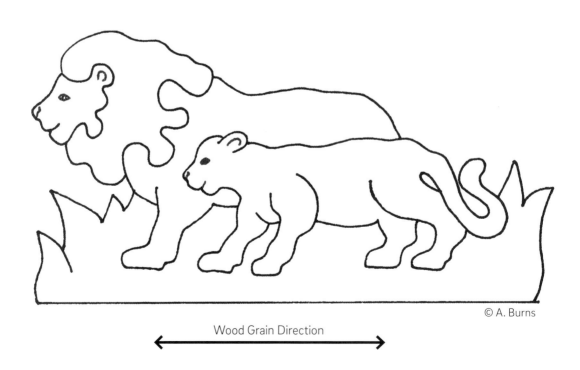

© A. Burns

Wood Grain Direction

←——————————→

Traveling Elephants

© A. Burns

Wood Grain Direction

Gentle Giants

Wood Grain Direction

© A. Burns

Deer in Glen

© A. Burns

Wood Grain Direction

Hoppy Bunnies

© A. Burns

Wood Grain Direction

Grazing Horses

Wood Grain Direction

© A. Burns

Kangaroo Pair

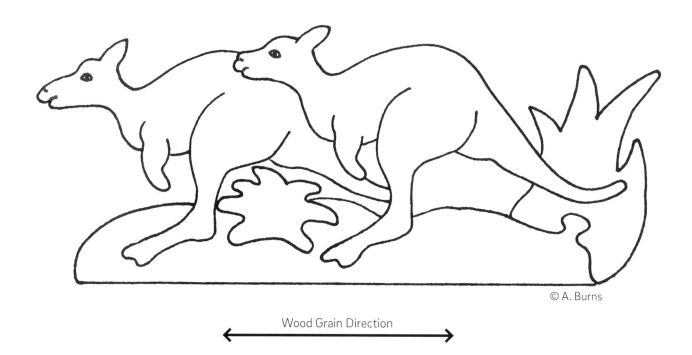

© A. Burns

Wood Grain Direction

Penguins on Ice

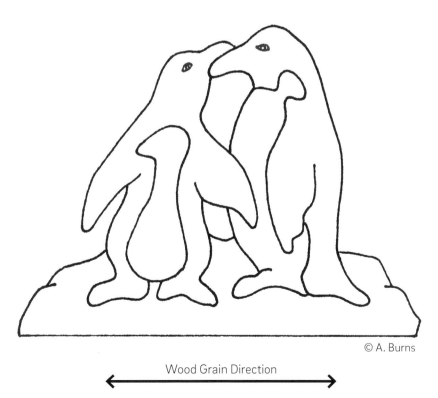

© A. Burns

Wood Grain Direction

Unicorns

© A. Burns

Wood Grain Direction

Turtle Family

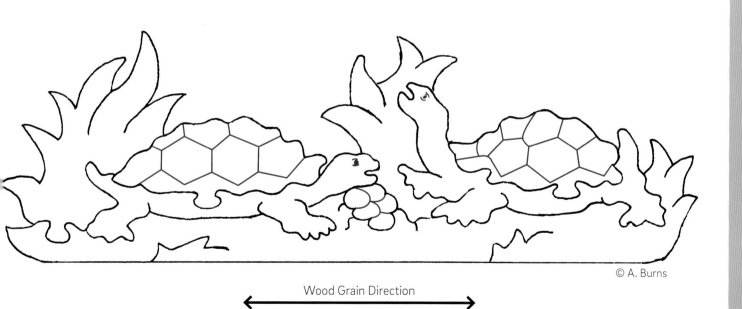

© A. Burns

Wood Grain Direction

Cypress Tree

Wood Grain Direction

© A. Burns

Animals

In this section, you'll find puzzles of creatures from around the world. We've included some of our favorite animals: camels, monkeys, hummingbirds, and, of course, puppies and kittens! As you scroll these puzzles, pay attention to the grain direction. There can be some delicate areas on the puzzles that could break if you cut against the grain. When you finish cutting, you can play with paint to easily change the look of these animals. Stand these puzzles alone or display them together to create a wild, wonderful animal kingdom!

37 Eagle in Flight

38 Flying Macaw

44 Baleen Whales

36 Ruby-Throated Hummingbird

48 Rainforest Frogs

40 Cats and Kittens

41 Pile of Pups

42 Pet Tropical Fish

43 Orca Whales

45 Beavers in Den

46 Fox Family

50 Camels in the Desert

52 Monkeys in a Tree

Ruby-Throated Hummingbird

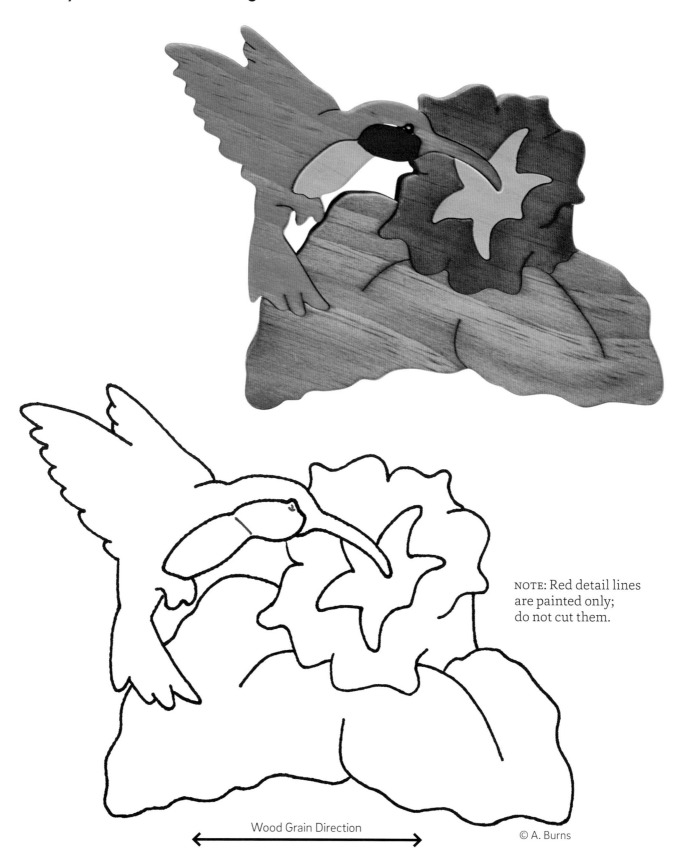

NOTE: Red detail lines are painted only; do not cut them.

Wood Grain Direction

© A. Burns

Eagle in Flight

© A. Burns

← Wood Grain Direction →

Flying Macaw

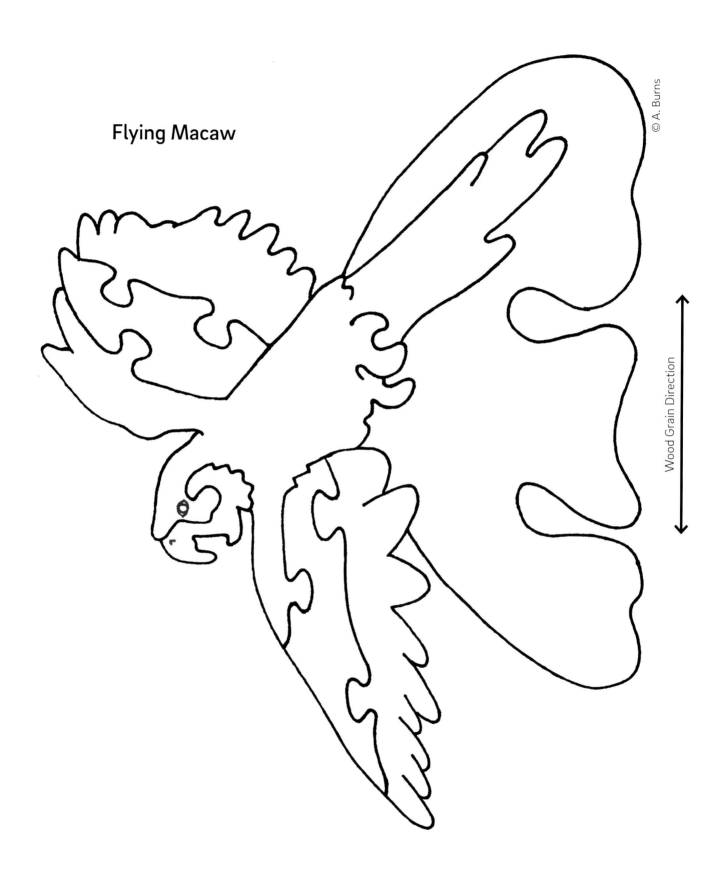

© A. Burns

Wood Grain Direction

Cats and Kittens

© A. Burns

Wood Grain Direction

Pile of Pups

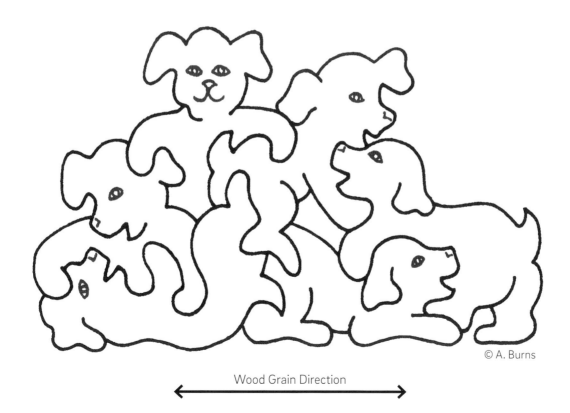

© A. Burns

Wood Grain Direction

Pet Tropical Fish

© A. Burns

Wood Grain Direction

Orca Whales

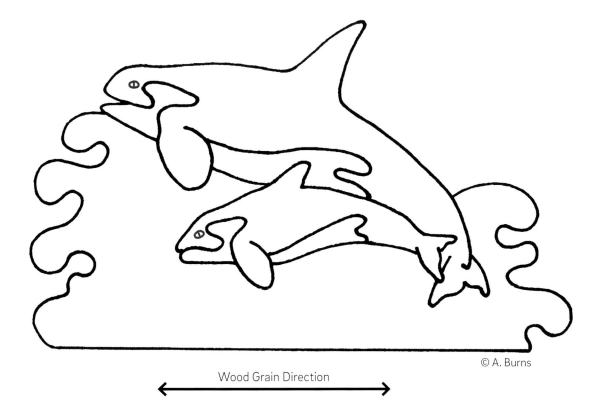

© A. Burns

← Wood Grain Direction →

Baleen Whales

Wood Grain Direction

© A. Burns

Beavers in Den

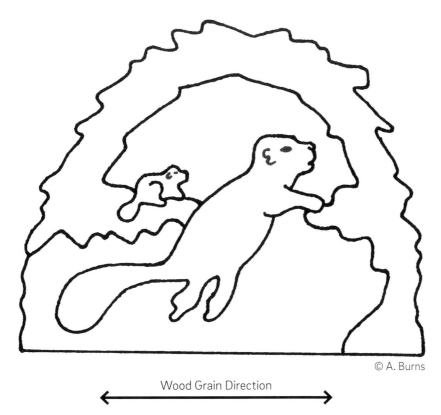

© A. Burns

Wood Grain Direction

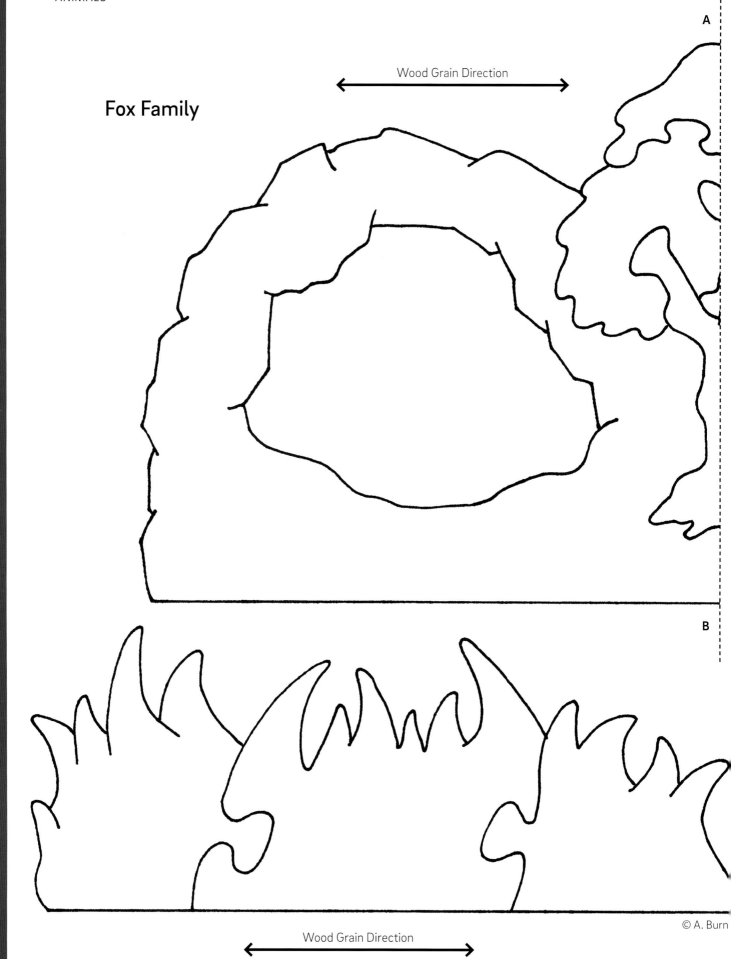

Fox Family

Wood Grain Direction

A

B

Wood Grain Direction

© A. Burn

A

© A. Burns

B

Wood Grain Direction

© A. Burns

Rainforest Frogs

© A. Burns

Wood Grain Direction

Camels in the Desert

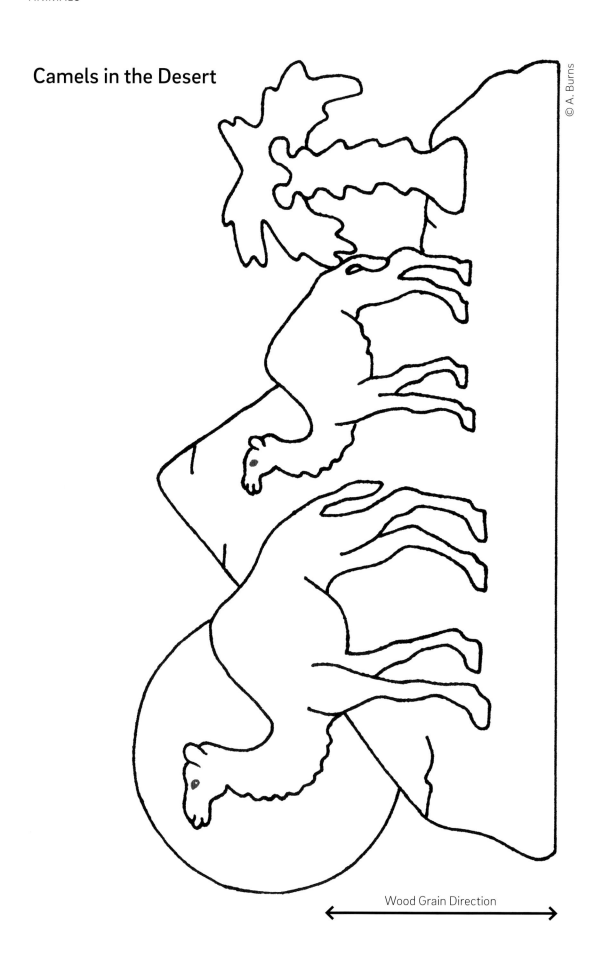

© A. Burns

Wood Grain Direction

Monkeys in a Tree

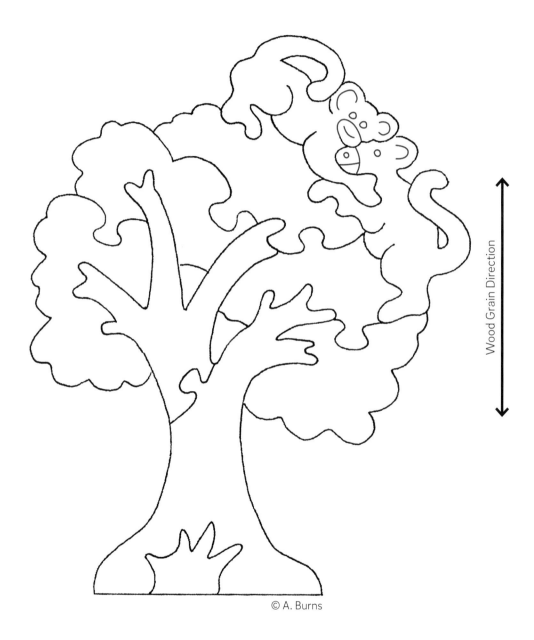

Wood Grain Direction

© A. Burns

Down on the Farm

We got a lot of inspiration for these puzzles from our childhood—we both grew up in western New York, surrounded by beautiful countryside. Among others, we included pigs, cows, chickens, a wishing well, fences, a barn, and of course the farmer and his tractor! When cut, the puzzles can stand alone or can be displayed together—creating a 24-piece barnyard scene!

A great way to display these puzzles is on a shelf, so we included patterns for brackets on page 88. Make sure to use wood screws or sheet rock screws to secure the shelf to the wall.

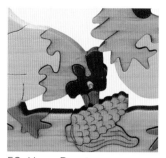

58 Hens, Roosters and Chicks

59 Hungry Chicks

65 Billy Goats Gruff

66 Three Little Pigs

72 Friendly Farm House

71 How Green is My Pasture

56 Farmer and Tractor

81 Outhouse

82 Chicken House

60 Cow Family

62 Moo-dy Cows

63 Mare and Foal

64 Bo Peep's Sheep

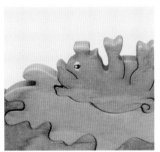

67 Splish Splash

68 Geese and Goslings

69 Playtime Pup

70 Haystack

74 Barn

76 Hay Wagon

78 Pickup Truck

80 Wishing Well

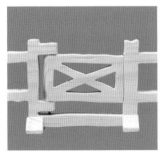

84 Fence, Single Gate
and Double Gate

86 Pine Trees

88 Rooster Shelf

Farmer and Tractor

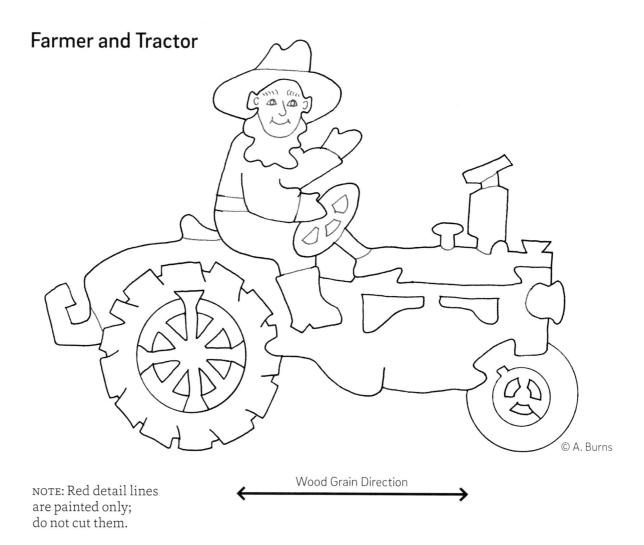

© A. Burns

NOTE: Red detail lines
are painted only;
do not cut them.

Wood Grain Direction

Hens, Roosters and Chicks

© A. Burns

Wood Grain Direction

Hungry Chicks

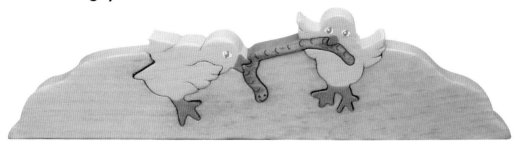

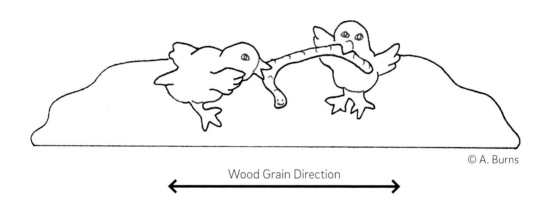

© A. Burns

←————— Wood Grain Direction —————→

Cow Family

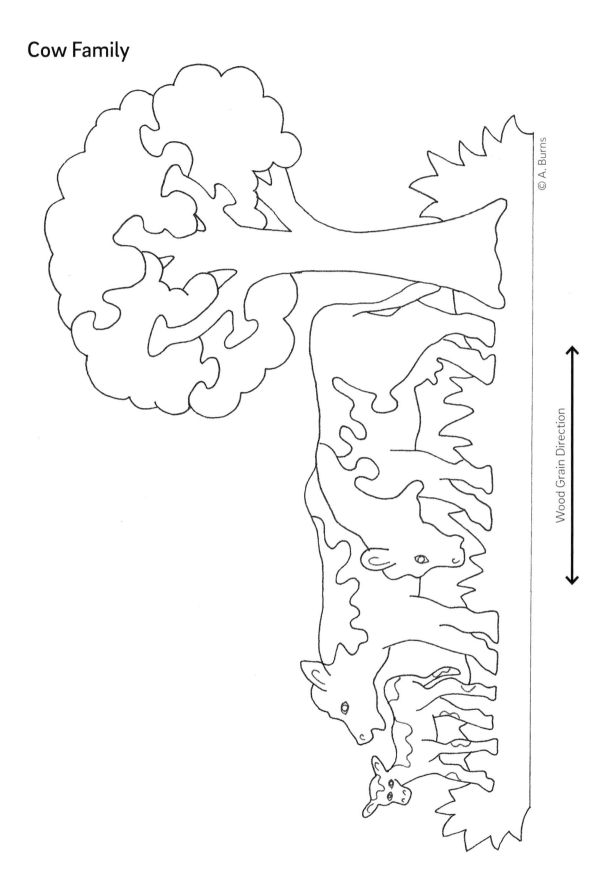

© A. Burns

Wood Grain Direction

Moo-dy Cows

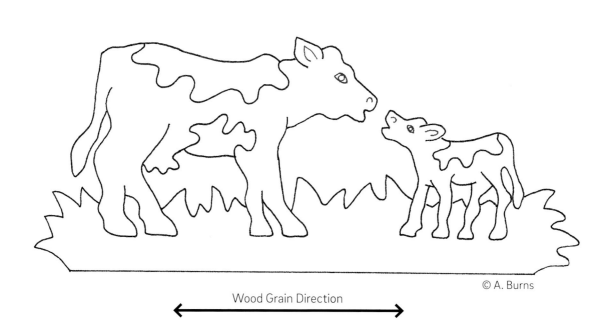

© A. Burns

Wood Grain Direction

Mare and Foal

Wood Grain Direction

© A. Burns

Bo Peep's Sheep

© A. Burns

Wood Grain Direction

Billy Goats Gruff

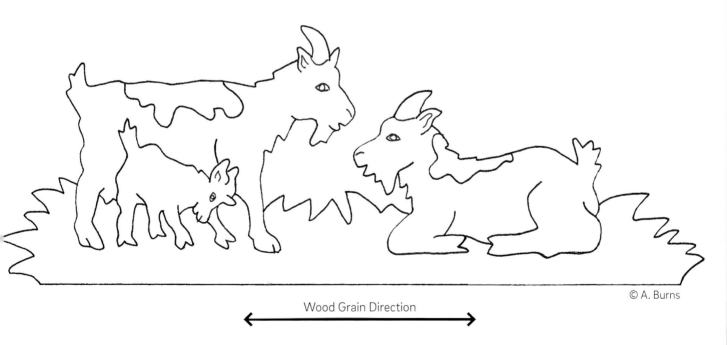

© A. Burns

Wood Grain Direction

Three Little Pigs

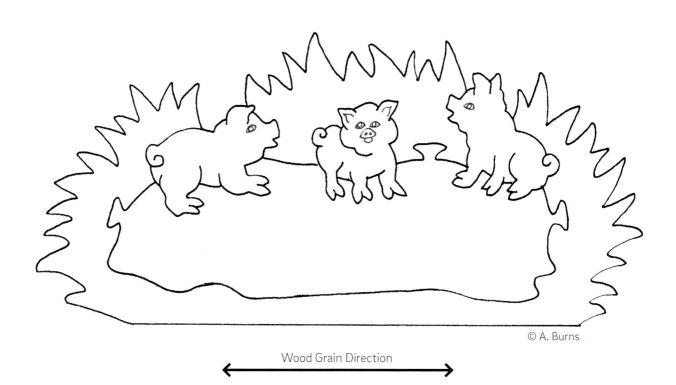

© A. Burns

Wood Grain Direction

Splish Splash

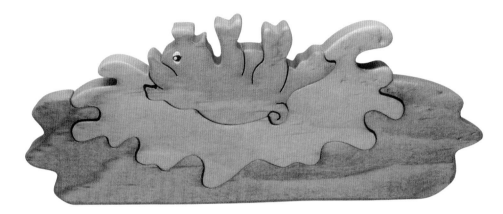

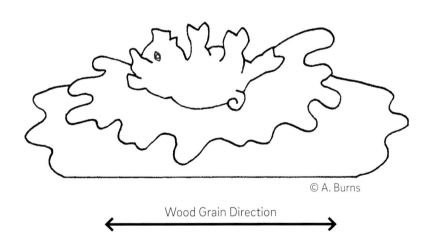

© A. Burns

Wood Grain Direction

Geese and Goslings

© A. Burns

Wood Grain Direction

Playtime Pup

© A. Burns

Wood Grain Direction

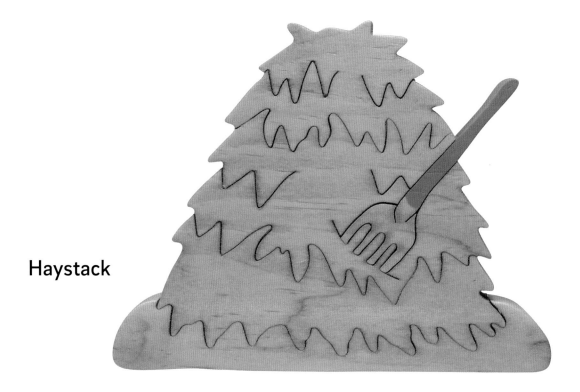

Haystack

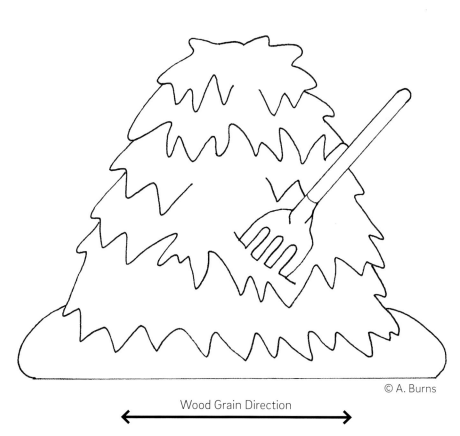

© A. Burns

Wood Grain Direction

How Green is My Pasture

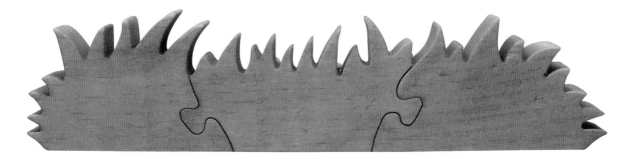

© A. Burns

Wood Grain Direction

Friendly Farm House

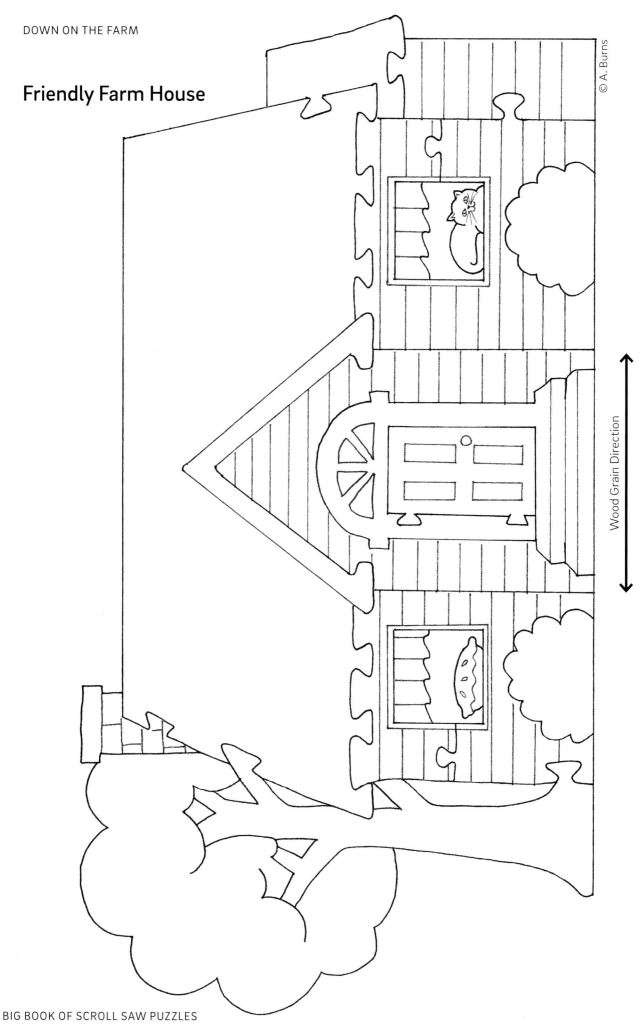

Wood Grain Direction

© A. Burns

Barn

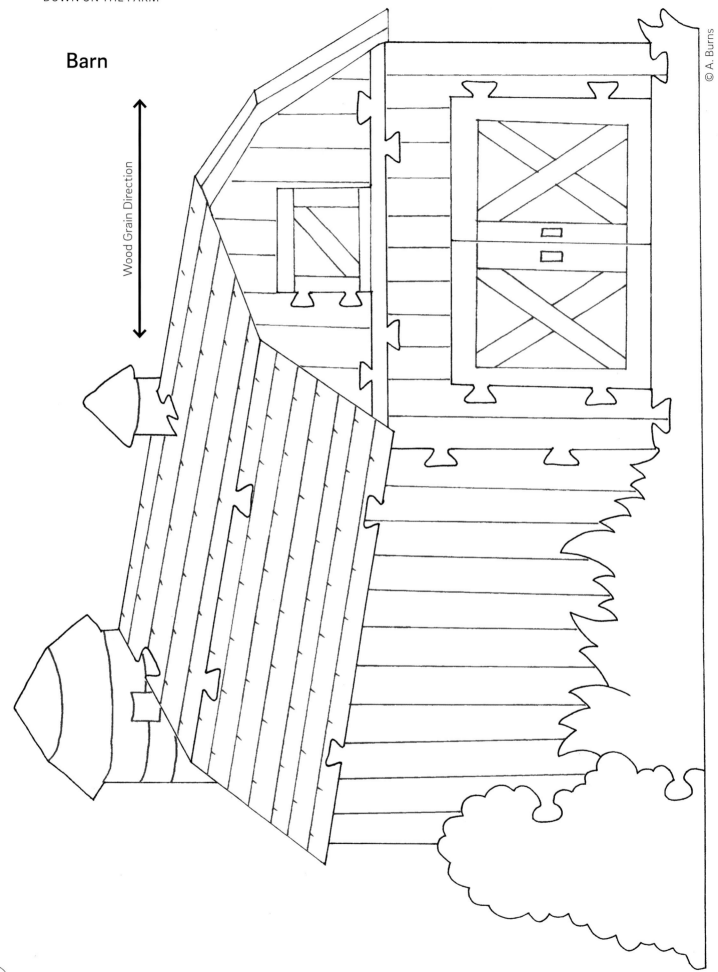

Wood Grain Direction

© A. Burns

Hay Wagon

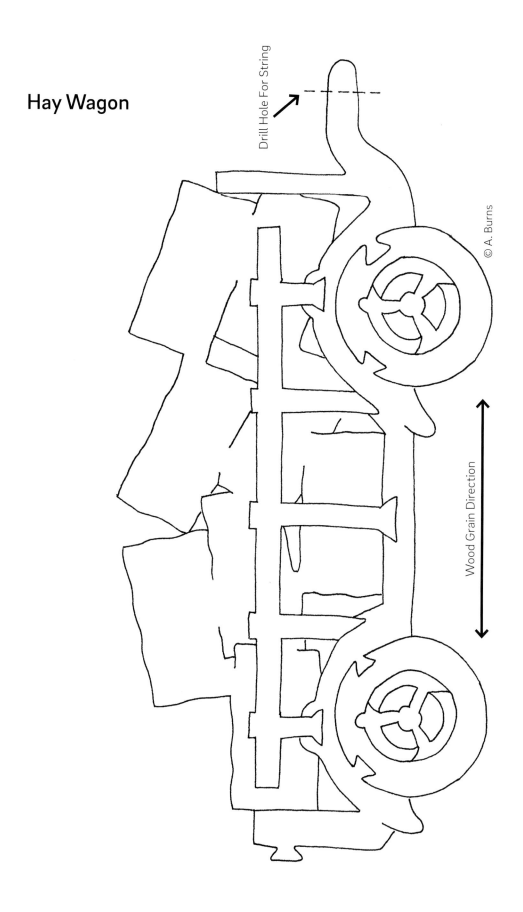

Drill Hole For String

© A. Burns

Wood Grain Direction

Pickup Truck

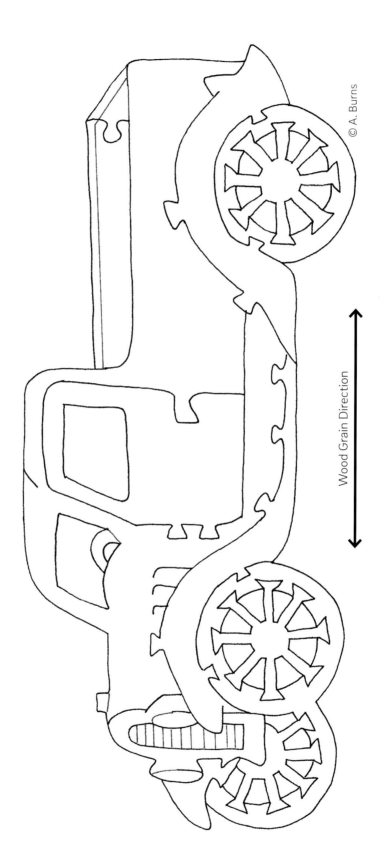

Wood Grain Direction

© A. Burns

Wishing Well

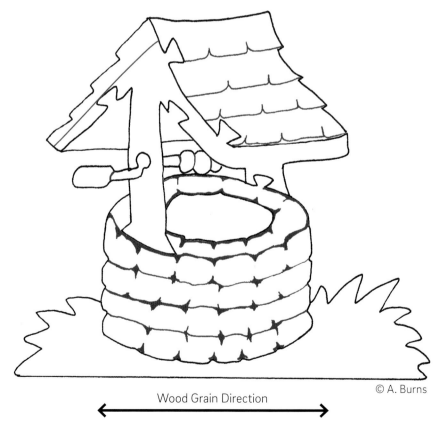

Wood Grain Direction

© A. Burns

Outhouse

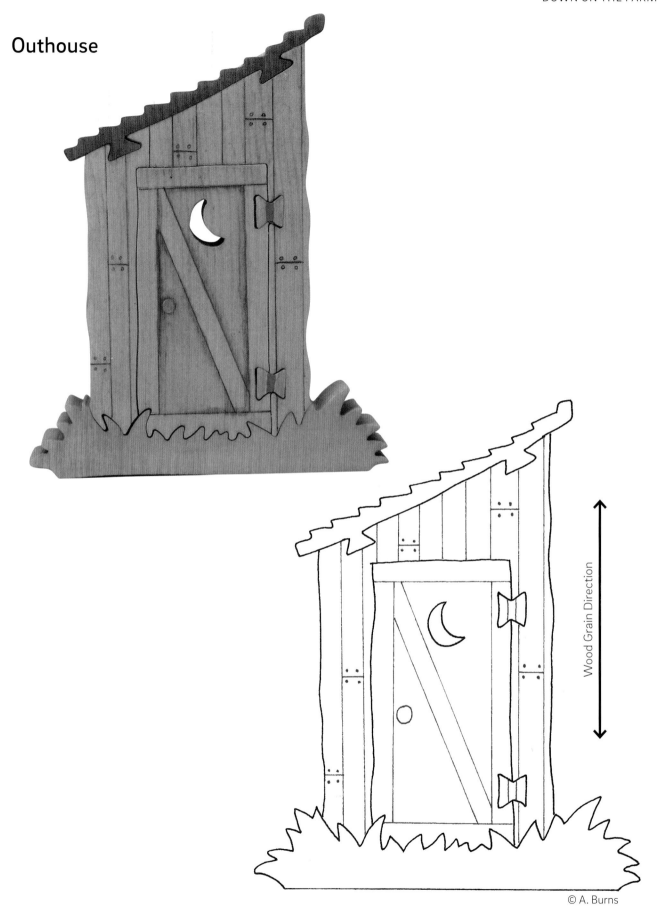

Wood Grain Direction

© A. Burns

Chicken House

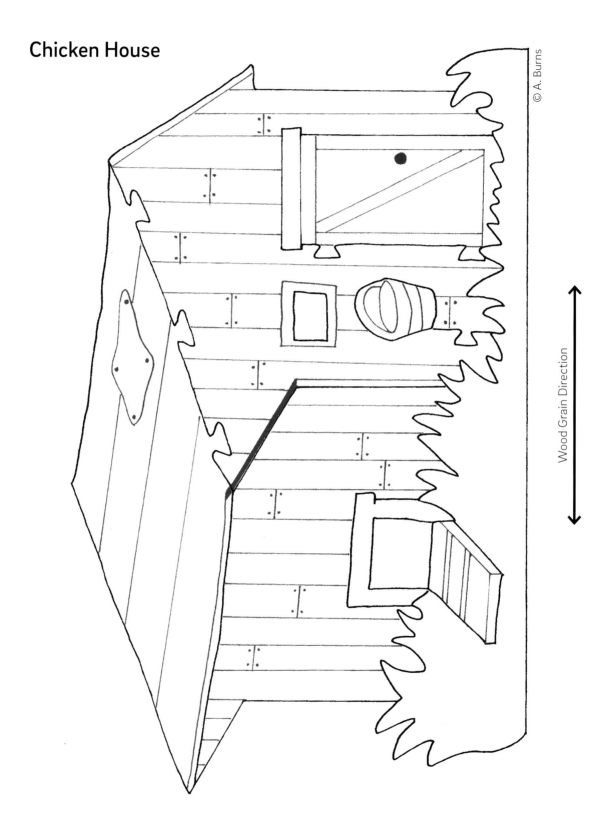

Wood Grain Direction

© A. Burns

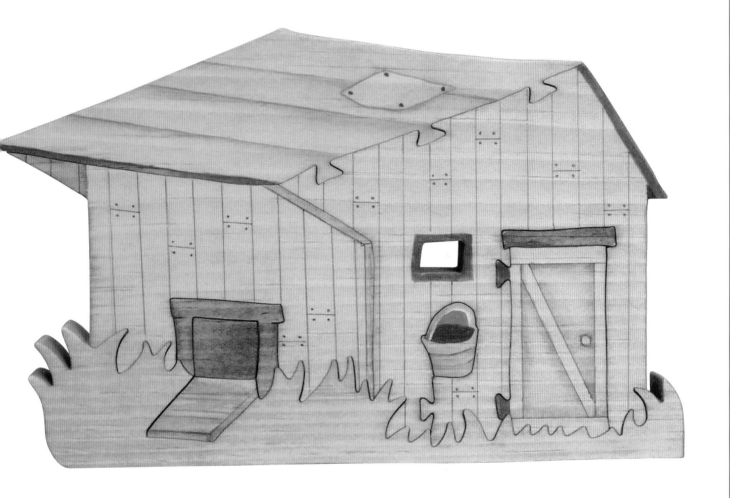

Fence, Single Gate and Double Gate

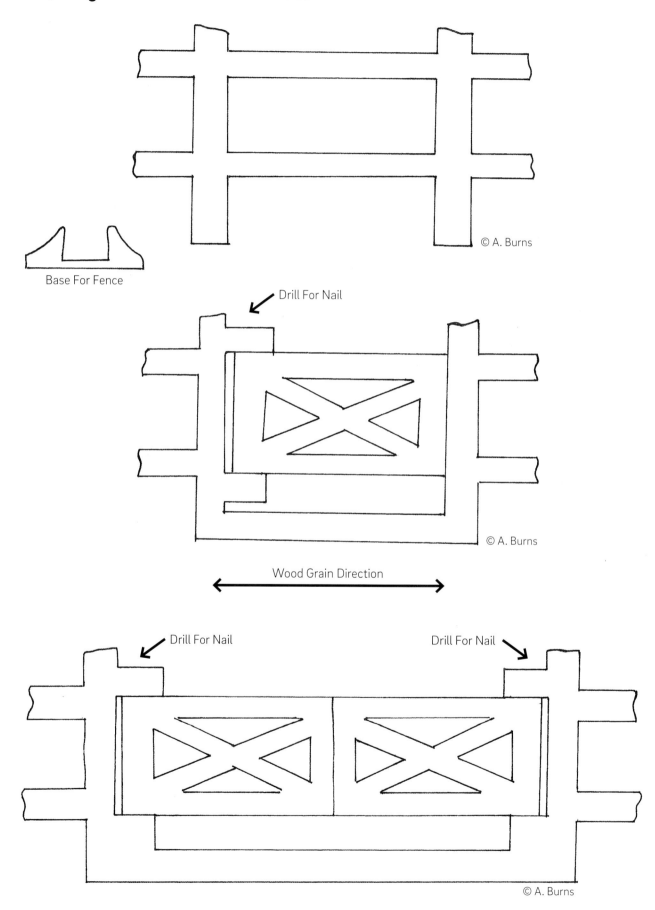

© A. Burns

Base For Fence

Drill For Nail

© A. Burns

Wood Grain Direction

Drill For Nail   Drill For Nail

© A. Burns

Pine Trees

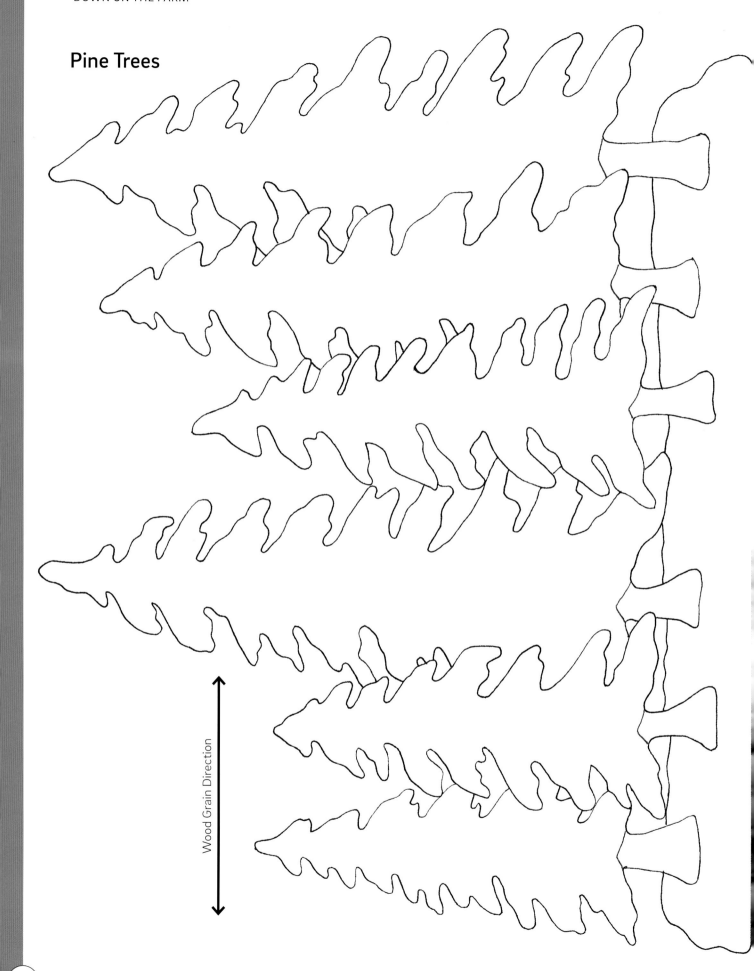

Wood Grain Direction

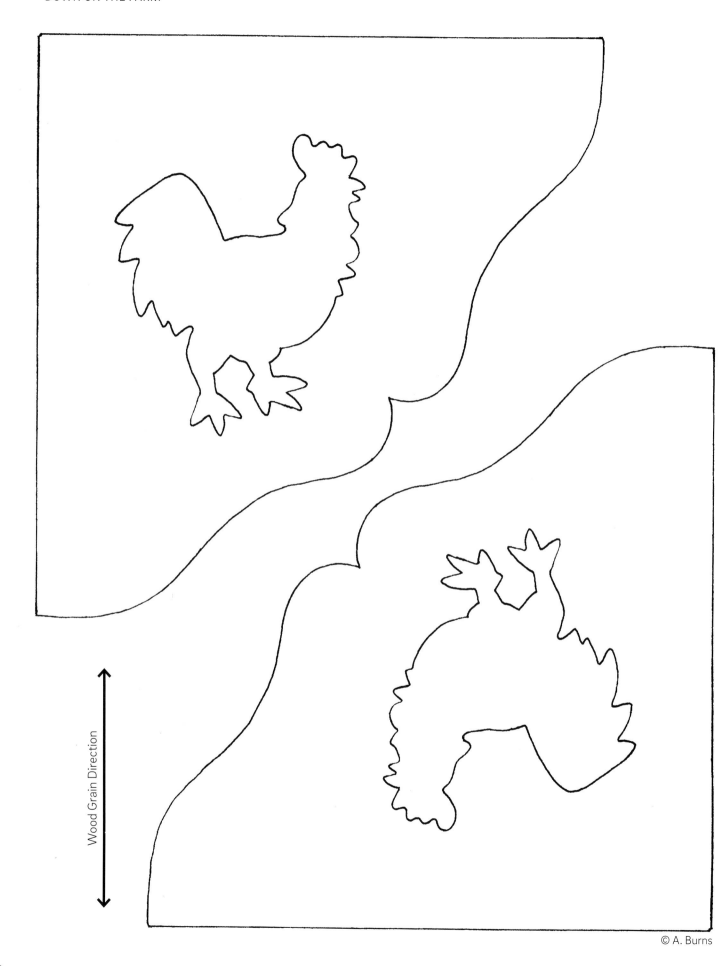

Wood Grain Direction

© A. Burns

Rooster Shelf

Holidays

You'll be scrolling throughout the year with this festive collection of puzzles. In this section, we included puzzles for holidays, seasons, and other memorable occasions. You'll find a rose for Valentine's Day, a snowman for winter, a cornucopia for Thanksgiving, a tree for spring, and a cake for birthdays, among others. Give these puzzles as gifts, display them alone, or mix and match them to create a display you can enjoy all year long. We hope these holiday designs will bring the joys of every season into your home.

93 Birthday Cake

94 St. Patrick's Day Leprechaun

100 Summer Flight

101 Star Spangled USA

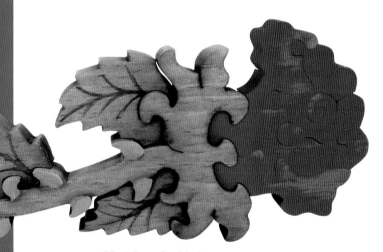

92 A Rose for My Love

108 Witch in Flight

110 Harvest Cornucopia

116 Chanukah Menorah

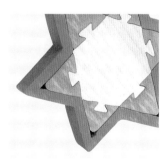

118 Star of David

95 Easter Bunnies in a Basket

96 Spring Tree with Birds

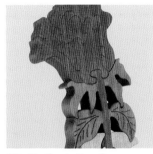

98 Mother's Day Rose

99 Number One Dad

102 Harvest Time Scarecrow

104 Maple Leaves

105 Peek-A-Boo Kitty

106 Ghost with Pumpkin

112 Autumn Wreath

114 Friendly Snowman

122 Santa of Peace

119 Snowflake

120 Guardian Angel

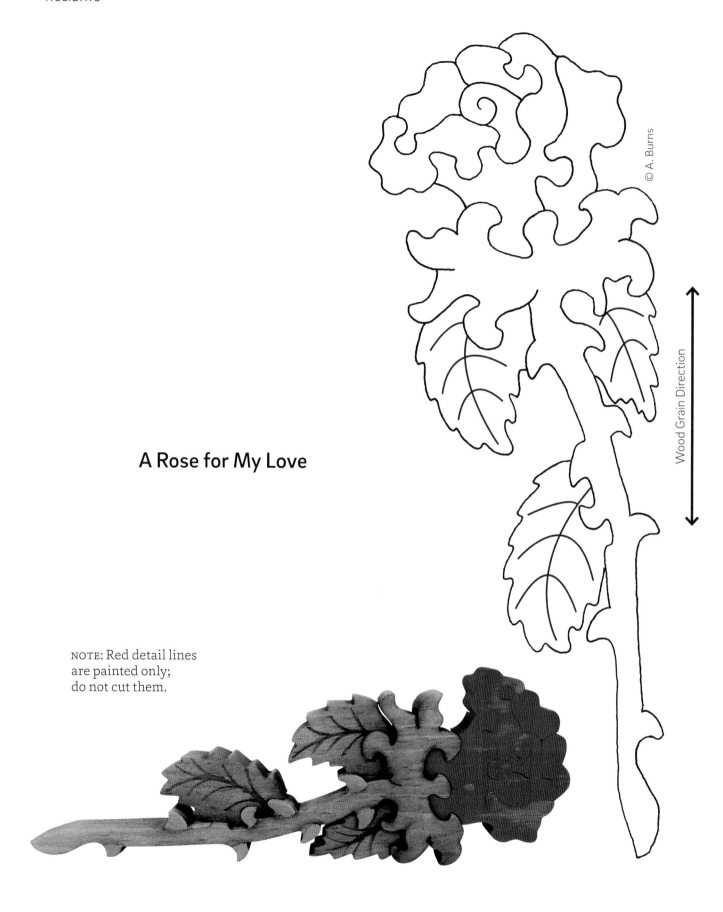

© A. Burns

Wood Grain Direction

A Rose for My Love

NOTE: Red detail lines
are painted only;
do not cut them.

Birthday Cake

© A. Burns

Wood Grain Direction

St. Patrick's Day Leprechaun

© A. Burns

Wood Grain Direction

Easter Bunnies in a Basket

© A. Burns

Wood Grain Direction ←——————→

Spring Tree with Birds

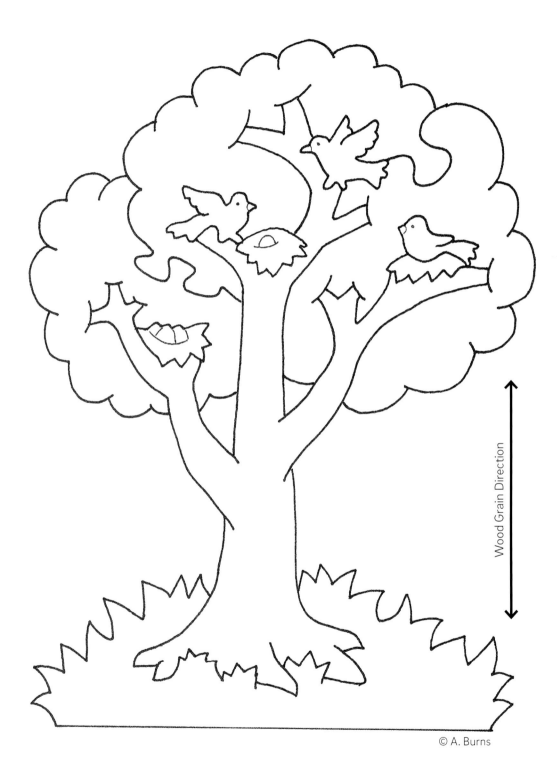

Wood Grain Direction

© A. Burns

Mother's Day Rose

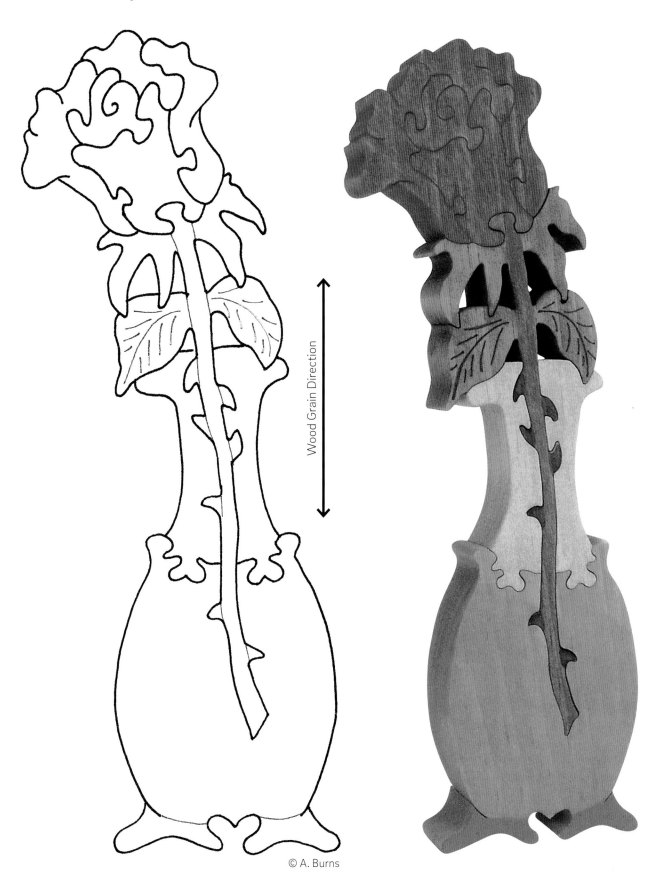

Wood Grain Direction

© A. Burns

Number One Dad

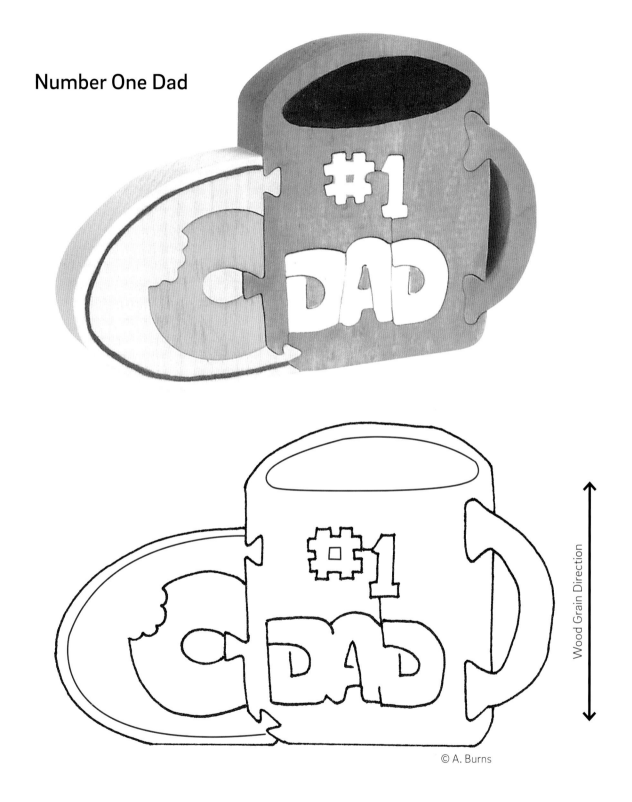

Wood Grain Direction

© A. Burns

Summer Flight

Wood Grain Direction

© A. Burns

Star Spangled USA

© A. Burns

Wood Grain Direction

Harvest Time Scarecrow

© A. Burns

Wood Grain Direction

Maple Leaves

Wood Grain Direction

© A. Burns

Peek-A-Boo Kitty

Wood Grain Direction

© A. Burns

Ghost with Pumpkin

Wood Grain Direction

© A. Burns

Witch in Flight

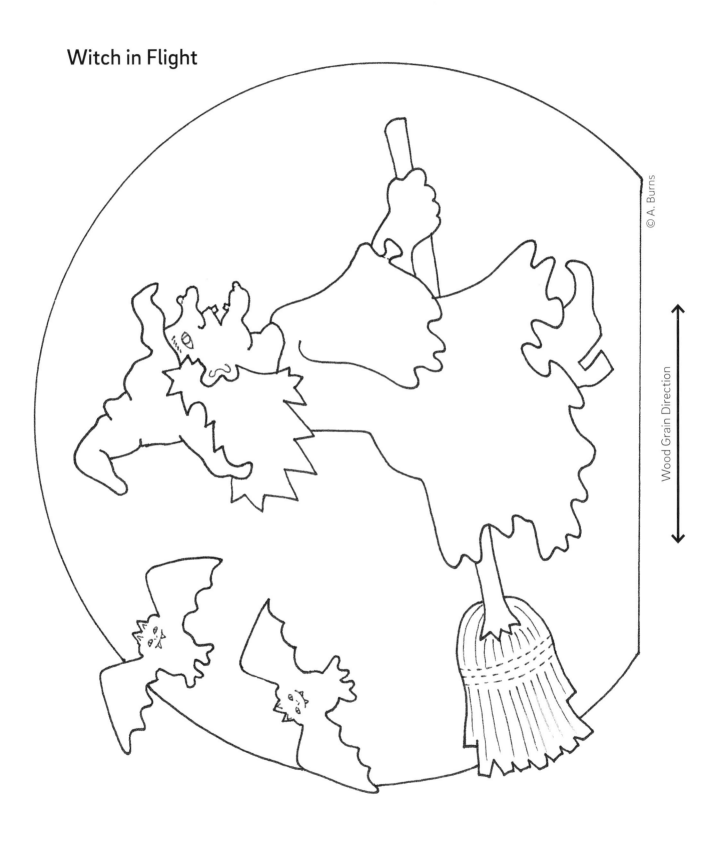

© A. Burns

Wood Grain Direction

Harvest Cornucopia

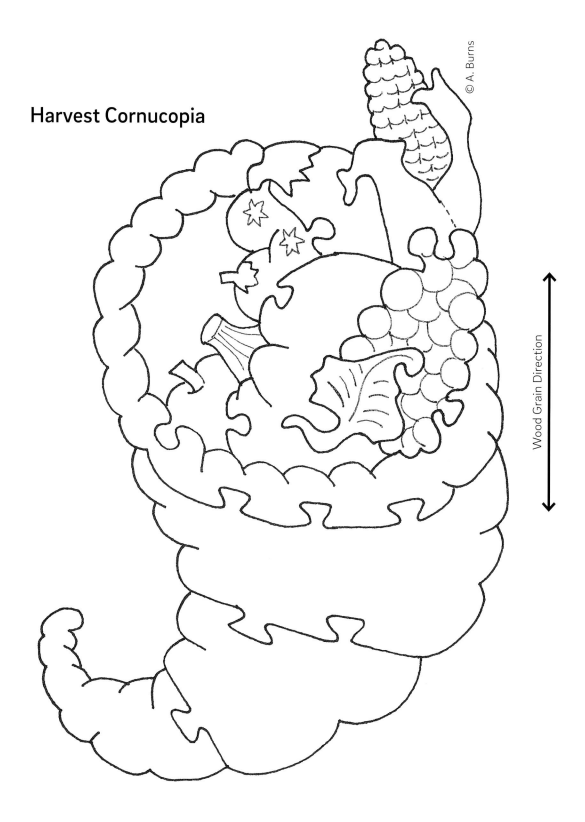

© A. Burns

Wood Grain Direction

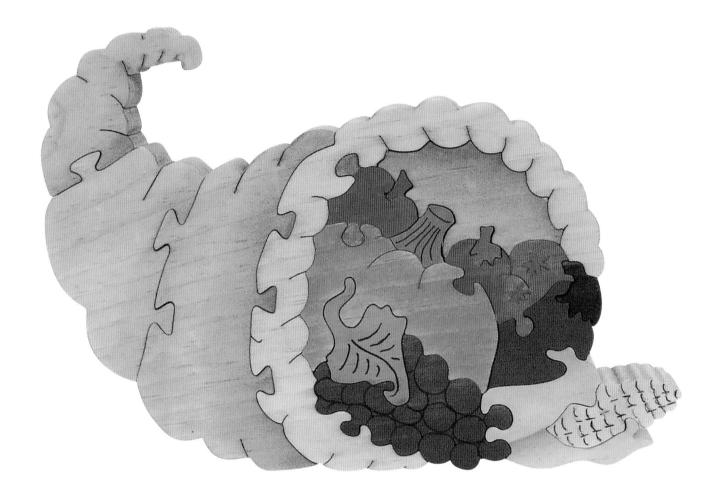

Autumn Wreath

© A. Burns

Wood Grain Direction

Friendly Snowman

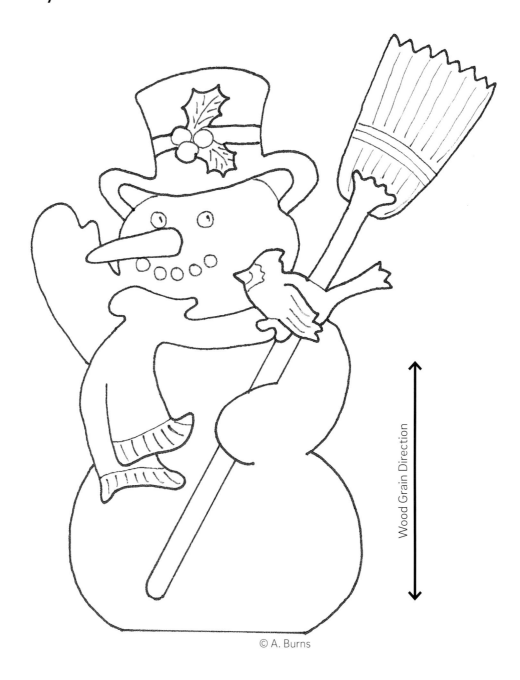

Wood Grain Direction

© A. Burns

Chanukah Menorah

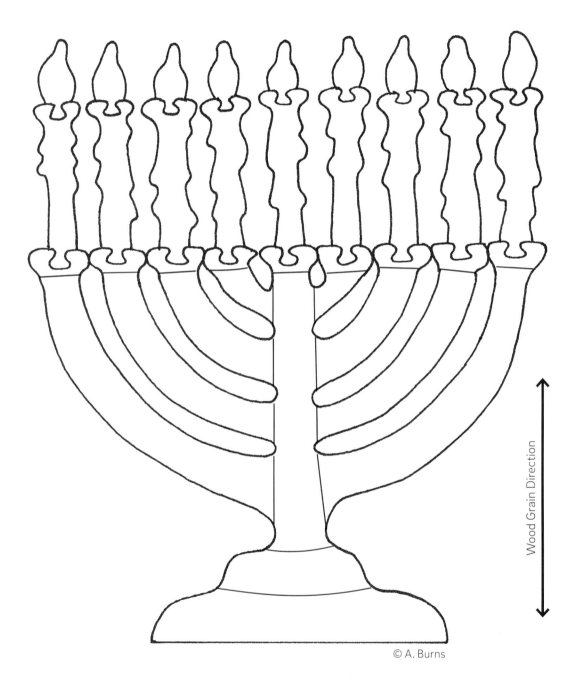

Wood Grain Direction

© A. Burns

Star of David

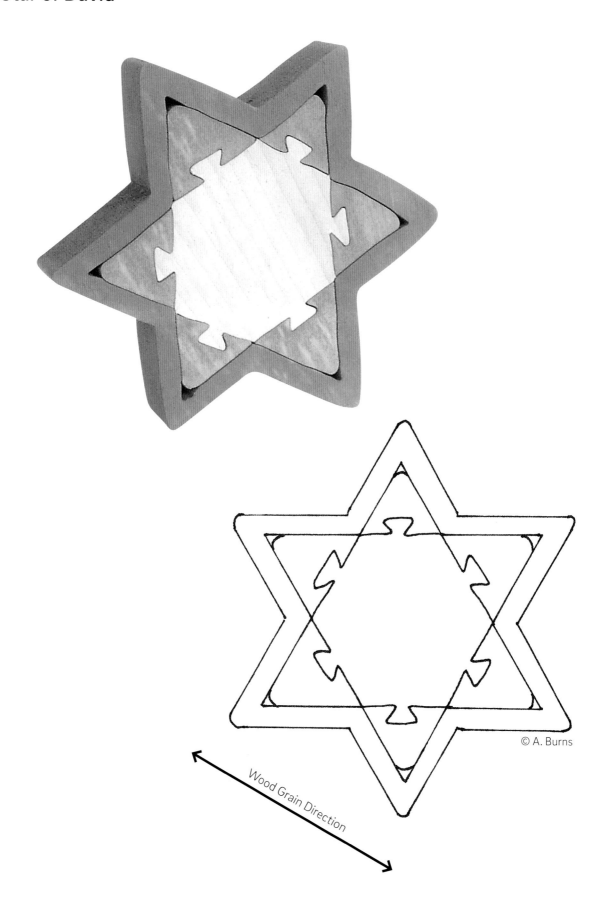

© A. Burns

Wood Grain Direction

Snowflake

© A. Burns

Wood Grain Direction

Guardian Angel

Wood Grain Direction

© A. Burns

Santa of Peace

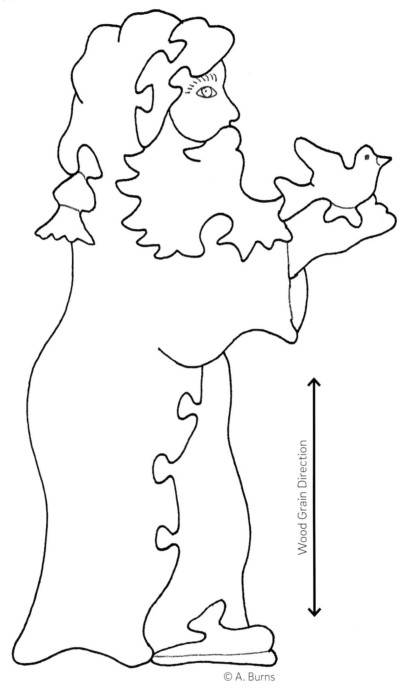

Wood Grain Direction

© A. Burns

RESOURCES

Resources

ADVANCED MACHINERY
P.O. Box 430
New Castle, DE 19720
www.advmachinery.com
1-800-727-6553

BEAR WOODS SUPPLY
139 Bonaventure St.
Cornwallis, NS B0S 1H0
Canada
www.bearwood.com
1-800-565-5066

BEN FINK'S WOOD SHOP
P.O. Box 84
Bainbridge, PA 17502-0084
www.bensscrollsaw.com
717-367-8064

TONY AND JUNE BURNS
4744 Berry Rd.
Fredonia, NY 14063-1502
www.scrollsawpuzzles.com

BUSHTON MANUFACTURING
HAWK WOODWORKING TOOLS
P.O. Box 127
319 S. Main St.
Bushton, KS 67427
www.hawkwoodworkingtools.com
620-562-3557

D & D WOODCRAFTS
654 Blue Ridge Rd.
Saylorsburg, PA 18353
www.dndsawbladesonline.com
610-381-2286

DELTA POWER EQUIPMENT CORP.
www.deltamachinery.com
866-999-1499

DEWALT INDUSTRIAL TOOL CO.
701 E. Joppa Rd.
Baltimore, MD 21286
www.dewalt.com
1-800-433-9258

ECLIPSE SCROLL SAW
11700 Lock Ln.
New Kent, VA 23124
www.eclipsesaw.com
804-779-2478
Limited availability

MIKE'S WORKSHOP, INC.
P.O. Box 107
Brandon, SD 57005
www.mikesworkshop.com
605-582-6732

OLSON SAW CO.
16 Stony Hill Rd.
Bethel, CT 06801
www.olsonsaw.net
203-792-8622

P.S. WOOD MACHINES
3032 Industrial Blvd.
Bethel Park, PA 15102
www.pswood.com
1-800-939-4414

SEYCO (EXCALIBUR SAWS)
P.O. Box 1900
Rockwall, TX 75087
www.seyco.com
972-722-9722

124 BIG BOOK OF SCROLL SAW PUZZLES

Request

We enjoy hearing from you. Send us questions, comments, and suggestions for future designs. You can contact us at *tburns10@stny.rr.com* or *artpuzzles@gmail.com*. We list events we participate in on our website, *www.scrollsawpuzzles.com*. You can find us on Facebook under the name Peachieoriginals. Please include a SASE if you would like a response to your mailed letter.

Contact us at:
  Tony and June Burns
  4744 Berry Rd.
  Fredonia, NY 14063-1502

Index

Note: Page numbers in *italics* indicate projects/patterns.